Vegan

THE ANTI-DIET APPROACH TO CLEAN EATING FOR CHRONIC ILLNESSES

HANNAH DIANE

@vegannahofficial

Contents

Intro...

If you're reading this book, my guess is you've tried a lot of diets. Maybe you've meddled in veganism* before, but you couldn't quite get past the nothingness taste of bland tofu. Maybe you've attempted diet pills, shakes, fasting, cleansing, or even (dare I say it) 'anti-diet' approaches that are just another diet in disguise. All to find yourself at the bottom of a tub of ice cream by the end of the week - feeling physically and mentally yucky!

Well, I'm not here to give you another diet, or to employ the scales as a measurement of your health, or even provide calories/macros/points alongside these recipes. Instead, the Vegannah philosophy avoids the 'all or nothing' approach that traditional diets thrive on, and instead allows you to tune into your body's needs and how you feel. Yes, I am giving you permission to adapt and change these recipes to best suit you. Most importantly, they all include natural ingredients from the earth to help you feel good inside and out.

Remember, you always have permission to eat whatever you desire, but ask yourself 'how will this physically make me feel?' And make your decision from a place of logic. We are all unique, and whether you live with a chronic illness or not, our bodies speak to us every day. We just need to listen.

*Refer to the definitions page for further information

So, take a deep breath...
And when you're
ready- begin your
life-long journey
to freedom...

Disclaimer

As you read through this book, I delve into my personal life and experience which includes reference to illnesses- both chronic and acute. Please be aware that I intend to share what has worked for me and am by no means suggesting this is a cure for all. Please do what is safe and healthy* for you, and always seek professional medical/mental health advice as needed. What is written in this book is not to serve as a substitute for medical care/advice and is categorised as opinion only. Furthermore, everything in this book is written without intent to copyright others and derives only from my own personal experience and experimentation in and out of the kitchen.

Additionally, I recognise the privilege I have in terms of food accessibility. However, I do reflect upon times my condition has left me bed bound, with such intense brain fog that cooking a meal was the last thing I could muster. Therefore, this book encompasses recipes ranging from 'easy' to 'advanced' (for those days you fancy a challenge), as well as utilising ingredients that are easy to obtain (most likely already in your cupboard or fridge- if not on the internet or in health stores). I specifically use as little ingredients as possible to make dishes that are not only natural and nourishing, but both affordable and easy too!

That all being said, I passionately believe in this philosophy and hope it brings you true health, freedom, and happiness as it did (and continues to do) for me.

*Refer to the definitions page for further information

About me...

At 27 years old, I was diagnosed with Myalgic encephalomyelitis/ ME (or often known as chronic fatigue syndrome/ CFS). Whilst this was heart-breaking and debilitating at best, I was relieved to finally have answers from the years of battling various illnesses and diseases. No doctor, it most certainly isn't 'just in my head!'. The majority of my life has included multiple hospital stays, referrals, medications, and various conditions ranging from Anorexia Nervosa* to Raynaud's Syndrome*, Irritable Bowel Syndrome*, Bulimia Nervosa*, Anxiety*, Depression*, Binge-Eating Disorder*, and Covid 19* to name a few. All of which I know now to have the potential to be caused and/ or hindered by CFS. However, I have always been active - running half a marathon only a couple of months before the 'final crash' (so named as it encompassed an array of difficult symptoms including episodic paralysis in my legs, being bed bound, and the eventual diagnosis of CFS at 27).

However, this is not a 'woe is me' story- in fact I intend for quite the opposite. Throughout my life, I have always been a perfectionist- always delving straight in to learning, growing, and building my lifestyle around health and wellness. Always with the intent to share the richest and highest quality knowledge with the world to help others. This has ranged from qualifying as a nurse and developing a career around paediatric mental health support- to committing to fitness instructing qualifications in my spare time, (and so much more). Yes, I get my finger in all the pies! Hours and days I have spent researching latest health trends, reading blog after blog on what is best to avoid/ eat to support chronic illness and live well. After all, we all want to live a happy, healthy, and long life, right?

*Refer to the definitions page for further information

The truth is I was burning myself out looking for the cure. For that magic ingredient that will make me 'healthier', happier, and live till 100 years old whilst still being able to do the splits. Little did I know that this relentless health-seeking was doing more damage than good, increasing my stress levels, and releasing cortisol* to keep my body's sympathetic nervous system (fight or flight response) in constant attack mode. When in reality, there is a much safer, easier way that is freeing and beautiful - one I intend for you to realise too. My perfectionism meant I was focused on black and white thinking; good/ bad, green/ red foods etc. Sound familiar? All the while, I was ignoring my body's signals and how I truly felt. At the depths of my diagnosis, my intolerance's and allergies were severely heightened. Therefore, I organically stripped back my diet to only include clean* foods from the earth (if I couldn't pronounce it, I wasn't eating it!). At first, I felt restricted and deprived, just like those dreaded 'diets' we've all done in the past. How come my friends can go out and enjoy pizza and I can't even leave my bed whilst I chow down this raw kale?

And then a wave came over me, why not pizza? So, in the huff that I was in, I ordered the pizza. Lone behold my stomach distended (which I frequently referred to as pregnant belly), became extensively painful, and an array of nausea gushed through me. That's why no pizza. Then it dawned on me. Instead of labelling this food as out of bounds, I reminded myself I could have it whenever I wanted, I just have to weigh out the consequences. Maybe I can make my own versions of my favourite foods so I can eat what I want and feel good too?!

Just like that, I began eating nourishing, delicious, natural, and healthy foods whilst never feeling deprived or restricted.
Vegannah was born, and I was free.

Love Hannah Diane x

Essentials

Once you get the staple equipment and ingredients (most of which are available at your local supermarket, health stores, or the internet), it becomes increasingly less expensive and habitual.

Here are some of my staples, many of which you will see multiple times throughout this book!

Equipment

- Good quality blender
- Saucepans/frying pans/woks
- Food weighing scales
- Measuring jugs
- Oven (including thermometer)
- Dining plates/bowls/cutlery
- Good quality juicer
- Baking trays
- Clingfilm and baking parchment
- Ice-cream scoop
- Mixing bowls
- Timer

Ingredients

MILKS: Almond, rice, coconut, oat, soya, hazelnut

NUTS: Almonds, cashews, hazelnuts, pistachios, pecans, peanuts

SEEDS: Chia, linseed/ flax, pumpkin, sunflower, hemp

FRUIT: Avocados, blueberries, bananas, mangoes, strawberries, raspberries, tomatoes, oranges, peaches, pineapple, grapes

VEGETABLES: Spinach, cucumbers, sweet potatoes, butternut squash, bell peppers, mushrooms, aubergines, courgettes, corn, carrots, beetroot

OILS: Olive, coconut, sesame, sunflower

BUTTERS AND SYRUPS: Maple syrup, agave nectar, peanut butter, cacao butter, hazelnut butter

BAKING: Cacao powder, coconut sugar, pure cane sugar, rice flour, tapioca flour, buckwheat flour, baking powder, oats, dried rice, rice/ buckwheat pasta, apple cider vinegar, spirulina powder, natural protein powder (soya), matcha powder, chickpeas, kidney beans, tomato passata, tomato puree, dairy-free yoghurt, dairy-free cheese

Breakfast

MATCHA PANCAKES!

- Serving size: 2
- Difficulty: Easy
- Time: 10 minutes

INGREDIENTS:
o   230ml rice milk
o   1 tbsp rice vinegar
o   100g rice flour
o   Half tsp matcha powder
o   1 tsp baking powder
o   1 tbsp vanilla extract
o   3 tbsp maple syrup (+ extra to serve)
o   1 tbsp vegetable oil
o   1 tbsp coconut oil (melted)

METHOD:
1.   Prep the milk mixture by adding the rice vinegar to the rice milk, mix, and set aside for at least 5 minutes.
2.   Meanwhile in a large bowl, mix together the rice flour, baking powder, matcha powder, and vanilla extract.
3.   After the 5 minutes have passed, add the vinegar-milk mixture, maple syrup, and vegetable oil to the large bowl and combine all together to form a batter.
4.   Use the melted coconut oil to line your frying pan before cooking your pancakes on a medium heat for approximately 2 minutes each side.

TOP TIPS:
Matcha has quite a strong flavour so adjust the amount of matcha powder by half teaspoon dependent on preference.

I prefer a ceremonial grade matcha powder for an all-natural taste!

Serve with a generous drizzle of maple syrup, dairy-free yoghurt, and blueberries for a delicious combination!

When cooking your pancakes, your pancake should display bubbles when cooking. Once this happens, it's time to flip your pancake and cook the other side.

WHITE CHOCOLATE AND RASPBERRY PORRIDGE

- Serving size: 1
- Difficulty: Easy
- Time: 5-10 minutes

INGREDIENTS:
o   40g oats
o   150ml coconut milk
o   100g of dairy-free white chocolate (melted and cooled slightly)
o   1 tbsp agave nectar/ maple syrup
o   Handful of raspberries

METHOD:
1.   On a small saucepan on the hob, warm the coconut-milk and oats together on a low-medium heat until simmering.
2.   Once the mixture is combined, remove from the heat, and add half the melted white chocolate mixture and agave nectar/ maple syrup.
3.   Once combined, heat again until desired consistency and serve with the remaining white chocolate drizzled on top and raspberries.

TOP TIP:
Dairy-free white chocolate can be found in most supermarkets and health stores.

SUBSTITUTIONS:
You can use almond milk rather than coconut milk for a less creamy texture if preferred- or oat milk for an even oat-ier taste!

WARMING WINTER PORRIDGE

- Serving size: 1
- Difficulty: Easy
- Time: 5-10 minutes

INGREDIENTS:

o 40g oats
o 150ml oat milk
o Half a medium-sized apple (cubed)
o 1 tbsp maple syrup
o Handful of sultanas
o 2 tsps of ground cinnamon
o Scoop of peanut butter (optional)

METHOD:
1. On a saucepan on the hob, warm the oat milk and oats together on a low-medium heat until simmering.
2. Once the mixture is combined, add the sultanas, maple syrup, 1 tsp of the ground cinnamon and half of the cubed apple.
3. Heat until desired consistency and serve with the remaining apple, cinnamon, and peanut butter.

SUBSTITUTIONS:
You can use almond milk rather than oat milk for a less creamy texture if preferred- or coconut milk for an even sweeter taste!

TOP TIP:

Ensure you constantly stir the oats and milk together when cooking to ensure it combines. If your mixture becomes clumped together or dry, try turning down the heat and adding a splash more milk.

PINA COLADA PORRIDGE

- Serving size: 1
- Difficulty: Easy
- Time: 5-10 minutes

INGREDIENTS:
o 40g oats
o 150ml coconut milk
o 2 tbsp desiccated coconut
o 1 tbsp agave nectar/ maple syrup
o Handful of pure dried pineapple
o 1 tbsp chia seeds (optional)

METHOD:
1. On a saucepan on the hob, warm the coconut milk and oats together on a low-medium heat until simmering.
2. Once the mixture is combined, add the maple/ agave syrup and 1 tbsp of desiccated coconut.
3. Heat until desired consistency and serve with the remaining desiccated coconut, dried pineapple, and chia seeds.

TOP TIP:
Ensure you constantly stir the oats and milk together when cooking to ensure it combines. If your mixture becomes clumped together or dry, try turning down the heat and adding a splash more milk.

SUBSTITUTIONS:
You can serve with fresh pineapple instead of dried if you prefer!

- Serving size: 1
- Difficulty: Easy
- Time: 5 minutes (+overnight/12 hours in the fridge!)

BLUEBERRY MUFFIN OVERNIGHT OATS

INGREDIENTS:
o   40g oats
o   Half a banana (mashed)
o   80g fresh blueberries
o   1 tbsp maple syrup
o   180g natural dairy-free yoghurt

METHOD:
1.   Mix all the ingredients together in a large bowl.
2.   Add the ingredients to an air-tight jar or container.
3.   Place your mixture in the fridge overnight or for at least 12 hours.
4.   Stir before enjoying!

• •

MIXED FRUIT OVERNIGHT OATS

- Serving size: 1
- Difficulty: Easy
- Time: 5 minutes (+overnight/12 hours in the fridge!)

INGREDIENTS:
o   40g oats
o   Half a banana (mashed)
o   80g mixed dried fruit (I use sultanas and cranberries)
o   1 tsp chai seeds
o   1 tbsp maple syrup
o   180g natural dairy-free yoghurt
o   1 tsp vanilla extract (optional)
o   1 tsp cinnamon (optional)
o   Fresh fruit and granola to serve (I use grapes, strawberries, and mango)

METHOD:
1.   Mix all the ingredients together in a large bowl.
2.   Add the ingredients to an air-tight jar or container.
3.   Place your mixture in the fridge overnight or for at least 12 hours.
4.   Stir before adding your granola and fresh fruit to serve!

STRAWBERRY AND CHIA OVERNIGHT OATS

- Serving size: 1
- Difficulty: Moderate
- Time: 10 minutes (plus overnight in the fridge!)

INGREDIENTS:
- 80g strawberries (chopped)
- 2 tsp agave nectar
- 1 small apple (cored and chopped)
- Small splash of boiling water
- 40g oats
- 1 tbsp chia seeds
- 120ml coconut milk
- 1 tsp cinnamon

TOP TIP:
If you'd like to add some additional protein- replace 10g of the oats with 10g unflavoured natural protein powder.

METHOD:
1. Blend together the strawberries and agave nectar to form a puree. Cover with clingfilm and set aside in the fridge.
2. In a small saucepan, heat the chopped apple with a splash of boiling water until soft. Set aside.
3. In a separate bowl, mix together the remaining ingredients to form the oats mixture.
4. Mash the soft apple mixture and add to the oat mixture- stirring well.
5. Place the pat mixture in an air-tight container in the fridge overnight (or for 12 hours).
6. Once appropriate time has passed, layer your overnight oats by adding a third of the strawberry puree to the bottom of your glass, and topping with a third of the oat mixture and repeating the layering process until all the mixture is in the glass.

PECAN PIE BAKED OATS

- Serving size: 1
- Difficulty: Moderate
- Time: 40 minutes

INGREDIENTS:
o   40g oats
o   1 flax egg
o   100g dairy free natural yoghurt
o   Handful of finely chopped pecans
o   1 tbsp maple syrup
o   Half tbsp cinnamon
o   Half tsp nutmeg
o   Half tsp ground ginger
o   Half tsp baking powder

METHOD:
1.   Mix all the dry ingredients in a bowl.
2.   Add the flax egg and yoghurt and mix well.
3.   Pour mixture into a lined baking dish for one.
4.   Cook in a preheated oven at 180c for 35 minutes approximately. (If your oven runs hot- cook at 170c).
5.   Ensure dish is cooked and cooled before enjoying.

TOP TIP:
You can make ground oats by blending regular oats to use if you prefer a cakey texture.

SUBSTITUTIONS:
If you want to add some extra protein- only use 80g oats and add 20g unflavoured protein powder to the dry ingredients.

FRUIT AND NUT PROTEIN GRANOLA

- Serving size: 6
- Difficulty: Moderate
- Time: 35 minutes

INGREDIENTS:
o   140g jumbo oats
o   1 tbsp ground cinnamon
o   6 tbsp coconut sugar
o   30g chopped mixed nuts (I use pecans and almonds)
o   50g dried fruit (I use 25g cranberries and 25g sultanas)
o   25g soy/pea/hemp protein powder (unflavoured or vanilla) mixed with 20ml water
o   Half ripe banana (mashed)
o   45ml maple syrup
o   30ml coconut oil (melted)
o   Half tbsp of vanilla extract (optional)

METHOD:
1.   Mix all the dry ingredients together and leave to the side.
2.   On a low heat on the hob, heat the syrup, coconut oil, and vanilla essence (if using) until liquid form. Remove from the heat.
3.   In a separate bowl, mix together the mashed banana and protein mixture and add this to your dry ingredients bowl.
4.   Add the syrup mixture to the bowl and mix well.
5.   Place the mixture in a lined baking tray and bake in a preheated oven at 180c for approximately 25 minutes (If your oven runs hot- cook at 170c).
6.   Ensure granola is cooked and cooled before enjoying.
Top tips!
Make sure to stir your granola halfway through cooking to get that granola crunch!
Store in an air-tight container to prevent the granola going stale and soggy.

TOP TIPS:
Make sure to stir your granola halfway through cooking to get that granola crunch!

Store in an air-tight container to prevent the granola going stale and soggy.

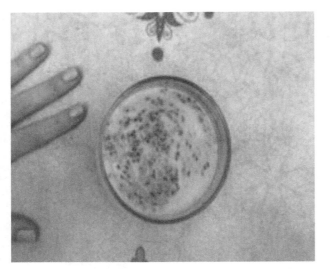

MANGO CHIA PUDDING

- Serving size: 2
- Difficulty: Easy
- Time: 5 minutes (+overnight/12 hours in the fridge!)

INGREDIENTS:
o   130ml coconut milk
o   2 tbsp chia seeds
o   Half large mango (chopped and frozen)
o   2 tsp maple syrup

METHOD:
1.   Mix all the ingredients together in a large bowl.
2.   Separate the mixture equally into 2 glasses.
3.   Place the puddings in the fridge overnight or for at least 12 hours.
4.   Stir before serving and enjoying!

RASPBERRY PROTEIN BOWL

- Serving size: 2
- Difficulty: Easy
- Time: 5 minutes

INGREDIENTS:
- o 150g raspberries (frozen or fresh)
- o 25g natural protein powder (unflavoured)
- o 100ml rice milk
- o 1 tsp vanilla extract
- o 1 tsp chia seeds

METHOD:
Blend all together and enjoy!

SUBSTITUTIONS:
If you fancy adding a stronger vanilla taste to the raspberry mix- switch your unflavoured protein powder to a natural vanilla one.

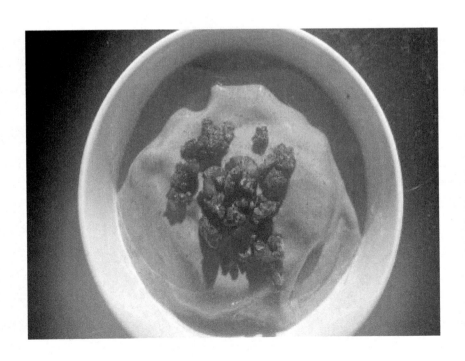

BLUEBERRY AND BANANA BOWL

- Serving size: 2
- Difficulty: Easy
- Time: 5 minutes

INGREDIENTS:
- 100g blueberries (frozen)
- 100ml coconut milk
- Half banana (sliced and frozen)
- 1 tsp chia seeds
- 1 tsp maple syrup

METHOD:
Blend all together and enjoy!

SUBSTITUTIONS:
If you don't have any chia seeds- feel free to substitute this with linseeds or flaxseeds.

SMOOTH AND REFRESHING MANGO BOWL

- Serving size: 1
- Difficulty: Easy
- Time: 5-10 minutes

METHOD:
1. Blend all the ingredients together and enjoy!

INGREDIENTS:
o   Half a large mango (cubed and frozen)
o   Half a large avocado (ripe)
o   100ml pure mango juice
o   100g dairy free natural yoghurt
o   1 and a half tbsp maple/ agave syrup

TOP TIP:
You can add a tbsp of oats to make this even thicker!

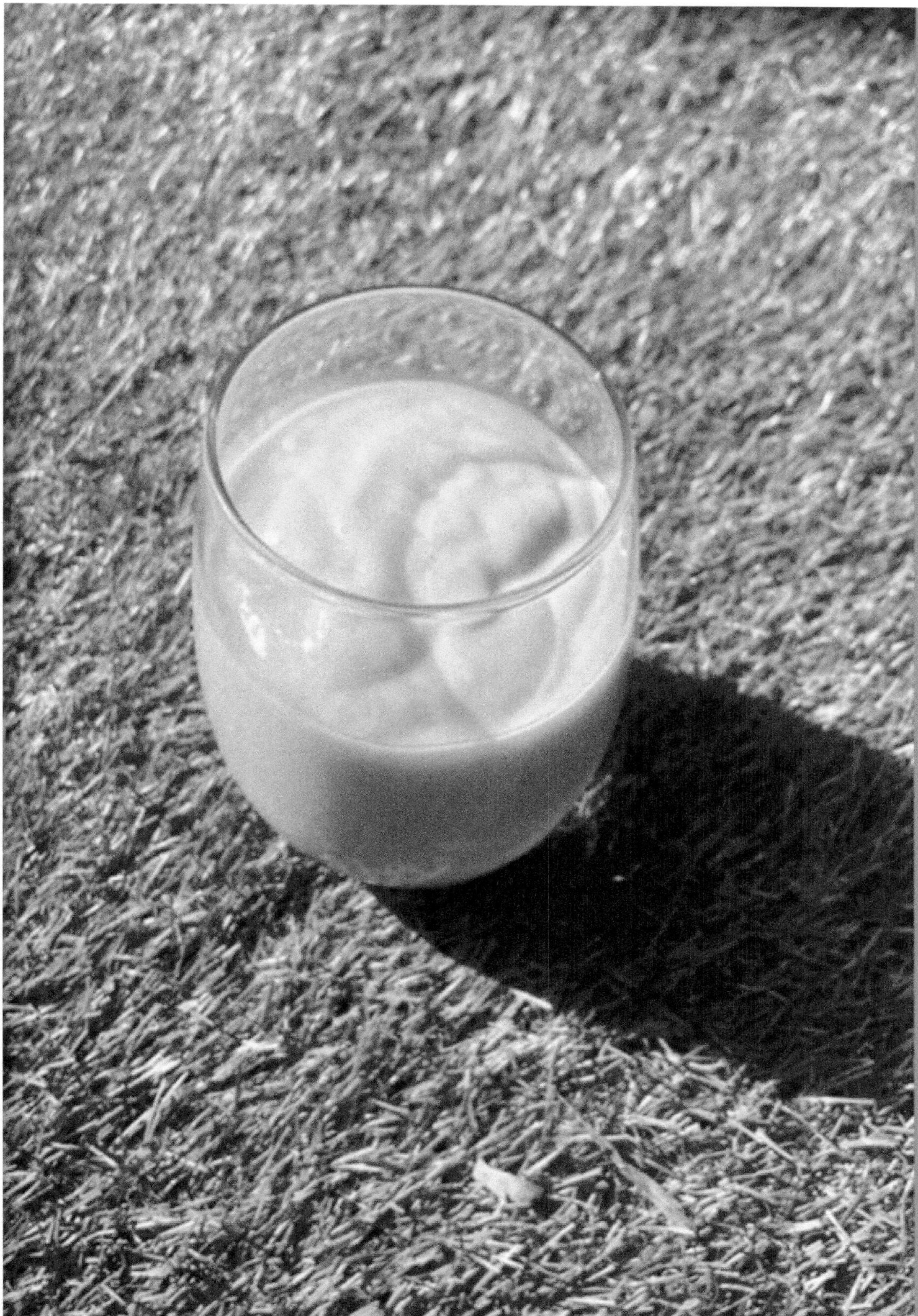

Mains

AVOCADO AND MANGO QUINOA SALAD

- Serving size: 2
- Difficulty: Easy
- Time: 15 minutes

INGREDIENTS:
- o 100g quinoa (+ 300ml water)
- o 1 large mango (diced)
- o 1 large avocado (diced)
- o Handful of coriander (chopped)
- o Handful of spinach (chopped)
- o 3 tbsp tamari
- o 1 and a half tbsp maple syrup
- o Juice of 1 lime
- o 3 tbsp sesame oil

METHOD
1. On a medium heat, add your water to the quinoa and cook the quinoa for approximately 12 minutes until all the water is absorbed and the quinoa is fluffy. Once cooked, allow the quinoa to cool in the saucepan.
2. In a separate bowl, create your dressing by mixing together the tamari, maple syrup, lime juice and sesame oil, and set aside.
3. In a large bowl, add your mango, avocado, coriander, spinach, and cooked quinoa and mix well.
4. Add your dressing to the large bowl and fully coat all the ingredients.
5. Season to serve as required.

SWEET AND SAVOURY PECAN SALAD

- Serving size: 4
- Difficulty: Advanced
- Time: 30 minutes

INGREDIENTS:
- Half a medium butternut squash (cubed)
- 100g of quinoa/rice
- 100g kale
- 80g chopped pecans
- 4 tbsp maple syrup
- Splash of olive oil
- 3 tbsp sesame oil
- 2 tbsp tamari
- 2 tbsp apple cider vinegar

TOP TIPS
For the pecan mix, make sure you are using a low heat and stirring consistently so they don't burn! This can be quite tricky!

I enjoy lots of dressing with my salads, but if you prefer it drier- reduce the apple cider vinegar, maple syrup, tamari and sesame oil by half when assembling the salad at the end.

METHOD:
1. Boil your quinoa or rice as per instructions and set aside for later.
2. Fry your butternut squash cubes in a splash of olive oil and season to taste. Once the squash has softened and appears golden brown, remove from the heat and set aside.
3. Make your pecan mix by placing the pecans, 2 tbsp of maple syrup and 1 tbsp sesame oil in a saucepan over a low heat. Consistently stir this mixture until the pecans are coated and at preferred texture, and set aside.
4. Assemble your salad in a large bowl by adding the kale, squash, pecans, quinoa/ rice, remaining maple syrup, sesame oil, tamari, and apple cider vinegar.
5. Mix thoroughly and enjoy!

FRESH VEGETABLE AND BEAN PASTA SALAD

- Serving size: 4
- Difficulty: Easy
- Time: 15 minutes

INGREDIENTS:
- 200g dried rice pasta
- 400g cannellini beans
- 100g cashews (soaked in warm water for 20 minutes)
- 5 tbsp nutritional yeast (plus more to serve)
- Approximately 100ml water
- 200g sweetcorn
- Jar of roasted red peppers (drained and chopped)
- 1 cucumber (diced)
- Large handful of coriander (chopped)

METHOD:
1. Cook your rice pasta as per packet instructions, drain and set aside to cool.
2. Place 300g of your cannellini beans, your soaked cashews, and 5 tbsp of nutritional yeast in a blender and pulse. Add your water conservatively and blend until you have a smooth consistency. You may find you don't need all the water!
3. In a large bowl add your pasta, remaining cannellini beans, sweetcorn, peppers, cucumber, and coriander and mix well.
4. Add your sauce to the bowl and mix well until all ingredients are coated.
5. Serve with a sprinkle of nutritional yeast if desired.

TOP TIPS:
Rice pasta is made from 100% rice and can be found in most supermarkets and health stores.
If your sauce is too thick, add a spoonful of water to loosen it up.

SUBSTITUTIONS:
You can use fresh peppers instead of roasted red peppers if preferred.

WARM VEGETABLE AND MISO RICE DISH

- Serving size: 3
- Difficulty: Moderate
- Time: 50 minutes

INGREDIENTS:
- 180g cooked rice of choice
- 1 large aubergine (chopped)
- 2 sweet potatoes (diced)
- 1 yellow pepper (chopped)
- 1 red pepper (chopped)
- Juice of 1 lime
- 1 tbsp of oregano
- Salt and pepper to season
- 3 tbsp sesame oil
- 1 tbsp maple syrup
- 1 tbsp rice vinegar
- 1 tbsp white miso paste
- Drizzle of olive oil

METHOD:
1. On a baking tray, scatter the chopped aubergine and sweet potato- drizzling the vegetables with olive oil, the oregano, and salt and pepper to taste.
2. Roast in a preheated oven at 200c (or 180c if your oven runs hot) for approximately 30 minutes.
3. Meanwhile, cook your rice as per packet instructions and set aside.
4. Make the dressing in a separate bowl by mixing together the lime juice, sesame oil, maple syrup, rice vinegar and miso paste.
5. Once the aubergine and sweet potato is cooked, remove from the oven, and add the chopped pepper to the tray- mixing well.
6. Coat the vegetables in the dressing and place back in the oven to cook for a further 10 minutes.
7. Once fully cooked, add your vegetables to your rice and mix well in the saucepan. Heat slightly until dish reaches preferred heat level.
8. Stir well and enjoy.

TOP TIP:
I use white rice as I find it binds together well creating a fluffy (and stodgy) texture that I love.

SUBSTITUTIONS:
If you don't have 1 yellow and 1 red pepper- feel free to mix it up with orange or green peppers. Although, be prepared that green peppers can make the dish a little bitter!
You can substitute white miso paste for brown or yellow miso paste.

BASIL AND CAULIFLOWER PESTO PASTA

- Serving size: 2
- Difficulty: Moderate
- Time: 20 minutes

INGREDIENTS:
o 140g cooked green pea pasta
o 250g cooked cauliflower
o 400g pre-soaked cannellini beans
o 30g fresh basil (chopped)
o 60g spinach (chopped)
o 300g pre-soaked cashews
o 250ml oat milk
o 50ml rice milk
o Sprinkle of garlic powder
o 2 tbsp nutritional yeast

METHOD:
1. Blend together the cashews, milks, and sprinkle of garlic powder.
2. Once creamy in texture, add the spinach and basil to the blender and blend again until smooth.
3. In a large saucepan, add the cooked cauliflower, cooked pasta and cannellini beans, mixing together.
4. On a medium heat, add the pesto sauce to the saucepan and stir through. Heat until desired temperature.
5. Serve with nutritional yeast sprinkled on top.

SUBSTITUTIONS:
You can use brown rice pasta instead of green pea pasta if you prefer.
You can also use 50ml more oat milk instead of 50ml rice milk if you don't have any rice milk.

TOMATO AND ROASTED VEGETABLE SPAGHETTI

- Serving size: 4
- Difficulty: Easy
- Time: 45 minutes

IINGREDIENTS:
- 1 and a half medium courgettes (diced)
- 1 and a half medium aubergines (diced)
- 1 red bell pepper (chopped)
- 2 tbsp sesame oil
- 200g dried rice spaghetti
- 300g cherry tomatoes (halved)
- 3 tsp paprika (smoked if able)
- 2 tbsp tomato puree
- 1 tbsp white miso paste
- 2 tbsp oregano
- Sprinkle of salt and pepper
- 2 tbsp Nutritional yeast (optional to serve)

METHOD:
1.   In a large bowl, mix together the chopped courgettes, aubergine, and bell pepper with the sesame oil and sprinkle of salt and pepper.
2.   Once coated, scatter the vegetables onto a lined baking tray and bake in a preheated oven at 190c for approximately 35 minutes.
3.   Meanwhile, cook your spaghetti as per packet instructions and set aside for later.
4.   Make the sauce by sautéing your cherry tomatoes in the paprika and cook in a wok on a medium heat.
5.   As the tomatoes soften, in a small bowl mix together the tomato puree and miso paste before adding it to the wok and mixing well. Reduce to simmer, add the oregano, and continue mixing to form the sauce.
6.   Once the vegetables are cooked, add them to the wok and fully coat in the sauce. Do the same with the spaghetti.
7.   Once all is coated in the sauce, heat until desired temperature and serve with nutritional yeast if desired.

SUBSTITUTIONS:
You can use brown miso paste instead of white miso if preferred.

TRIPLE VEGGIE PIZZA!

- Serving size: 8 slices
- Difficulty: Moderate
- Time: 25 minutes

INGREDIENTS:
o   240g sweet potato (boiled and mashed)
o   120g rice flour
o   40g tapioca flour
o   1 tsp baking powder
o   75g natural vegan cheese (grated)
o   1 tbsp nutritional yeast
o   75g mushrooms (chopped)
o   2 tbsp natural tomato puree
o   Handful of fresh coriander (chopped)

METHOD:
1.   In a large bowl, mix together the mashed potato, rice flour, tapioca flour and baking powder until the mixture is all formed together into a dough, and knead well.
2.   With a rolling pin, roll out the dough to desired shape and size and place onto a lined pizza/baking tray.
3.   Bake your pizza base in a preheated oven at 190c for 10 minutes and remove from the oven to cool only slightly.
4.   In a small bowl, mix together the cheese, nutritional yeast, and mushrooms. Set aside.
5.   On the pizza base, spread over the tomato puree, and sprinkle over the cheese and mushroom mix before putting in the oven to bake for another 12 minutes approximately.
6.   Remove from the oven and garnish with chopped coriander to serve.

TOP TIPS:
I would suggest not having your pizza thicker than 1cm and no thinner than 0.8cm to ensure it bakes well.
When kneading your dough, if your dough appears too sticky- add a little bit of water. If the dough appears too dry- add a bit more rice flour.
If you choose to add more toppings- your pizza will take longer to bake in section 4! Subsequently, if you add less toppings, your pizza may take less time to bake also- so keep an eye on it!

SUBSTITUTIONS:
Switch out the mushrooms for whatever toppings you desire- or add extra cheese instead for a margherita pizza!

MILD MIXED LENTIL DAHL

- Serving size: 2
- Difficulty: Moderate
- Time: 35 minutes

INGREDIENTS:
o   Splash of olive oil
o   50g red lentils
o   50g yellow lentils
o   50g green lentils
o   1 large tomato (finely chopped)
o   Sprinkle of salt and pepper
o   2 teaspoons of paprika (smoked if available)
o   Half tsp ground cumin
o   1 teaspoon curry powder
o   400ml coconut milk teaspoon of chilli powder or chilli flakes instead.

METHOD:
1.   Mix together your spices in a small bowl and set aside.
2.   On a medium heat fry your chopped tomato in a splash of olive oil, adding salt and pepper to taste.
3.   Once the tomato has softened, add your spice mix and stir well.
4.   Add all your lentils and coconut milk and bring it to boil. Mix well.
5.   Once boiling, reduce the heat to allow the mix to simmer on a low heat. Leave the dish to simmer for approximately 30 minutes-1 hour depending on preferred texture. It is essential to keep an eye on your dish every 5-10 minutes, stirring it occasionally to prevent it drying out!
6.   Add additional seasoning to taste, and serve!

TOP TIP:
This dahl is just gorgeous served with some dairy-free natural yoghurt and my simple side salad!

SUBSTITUTIONS:
If you want to add some more spice to your dahl, half the paprika and add a teaspoon of chilli powder or chilli flakes instead.

SQUASH, SWEET POTATO, AND COCONUT CURRY

- Serving size: 4
- Difficulty: Advanced
- Time: 75 minutes

INGREDIENTS:
o   800ml coconut milk
o   800g chopped tomatoes
o   Thumb sized piece of fresh ginger (finely chopped)
o   500g butternut squash (cubed)
o   500g sweet potato (diced)
o   Large handful of coriander (finely chopped) plus extra to serve
o   400g chickpeas (pre-soaked)
o   3 heaped tsp brown miso paste
o   Salt and pepper to season

METHOD:
1.   Heat the coconut milk, chopped tomatoes and ginger in a large saucepan until boiling. Season with salt and pepper to taste.
2.   Once boiling, add the butternut squash and sweet potato to the pan and stir well.
3.   Transfer to an oven dish and place in a preheated oven at 200c (180c if your oven runs hot)) for half an hour.
4.   Add the miso paste, chickpeas and coriander and stir well. Heat again in the oven for approximately 30 minutes.
5.   Serve with fresh coriander or coconut rice for a fuller flavour!

GREEN THAI CURRY

- Serving size: 4
- Difficulty: Advanced
- Time: 30 minutes

INGREDIENTS:

FOR THE PASTE:
- o   2 small green chillies (finely chopped)
- o   2 lemongrass stems (finely chopped)
- o   2 tbsp root ginger (finely chopped)
- o   3 small cloves of garlic (finely chopped)
- o   2 tsp of lime zest
- o   1 tsp ground coriander
- o   1 tsp ground cumin
- o   1 quarter tsp of pepper
- o   1 quarter tsp turmeric
- o   1 large handful of fresh coriander (chopped)
- o   1 tsp garam masala

FOR THE SAUCE:
- o   400ml coconut milk
- o   1 and a half courgettes (diced)
- o   200g mangetout
- o   200g baby corns
- o   Handful of broccolis (chopped)
- o   Handful of chestnut mushrooms (chopped)
- o   Drizzle of olive oil

TOP TIPS:
If you prefer a milder curry-reduce the quantity of green chillies or omit them altogether.

You can keep the remaining curry paste covered in the fridge to use within 2-3 days.

METHOD:

1.   Blend together all the paste ingredients and set aside for later.

2.   Add the courgettes, mangetout, corns, broccolis, and mushrooms to a large wok on a medium heat with the drizzle of olive oil until they begin to soften.

3.   Add 4 heaped tablespoons of your curry paste to the wok and coat the vegetables well.

4.   Add the coconut milk to the pan and mix well until fully combined. Bring to boil and then reduce to simmer.

5.   Heat until desired temperature and the curry has thickened before serving.

VEGGIE TIKKA FOR A TRIBE

- Serving size: 6
- Difficulty: Advanced
- Time: 1 hour

INGREDIENTS:
- o 1 tsp cumin seeds (blended)
- o 1 tsp coriander seeds (blended)
- o 1 tsp garam masala
- o 30g ginger root (finely chopped)
- o Half a tsp ground turmeric
- o 30ml sunflower oil
- o 1 tbsp tamarind puree
- o 2 tbsp tomato puree
- o 1 and a half tbsp paprika
- o Handful of coriander (chopped)
- o 1 medium sweet potato (diced)
- o 1 medium white potato (diced)
- o 1 medium butternut squash (diced)
- o 1 aubergine (diced)
- o 2 red peppers (diced)
- o Handful of baby corn (chopped)
- o 400g chickpeas (pre-soaked)
- o 800ml tomato passata
- o 400ml coconut milk

METHOD:
1. Blend together the cumin seeds, coriander seeds, garam masala, turmeric, half the ginger root, sunflower oil, tamarind puree, tomato puree, paprika and coriander until it forms a smooth curry paste.
2. Coat the potatoes, squash, aubergine, peppers, and baby corn in 2 tbsp of the paste, and evenly spread the vegetables on a lined baking tray before roasting in a preheated oven at 190c for approximately 45 minutes.
3. Meanwhile, in a large pan on a medium heat fry the remaining ginger root before adding 4 tbsp of the paste, coconut milk, and passata- stirring well for approximately 2 minutes. Bring to a simmer and lower the heat.
4. Once the vegetables are roasted, add them to the sauce with the chickpeas. On a medium heat, heat the curry until desired temperature to serve.

TOP TIP:
This curry recipe is so diverse you can use up any of those vegetables you have left in the fridge! Why not try adding some carrot, beans or peas?

47

Sweet treats

DOUBLE CHOCOLATE AND BANANA FUDGE CAKE

- Serving size: 12
- Difficulty: Advanced
- Time: 55 minutes

INGREDIENTS:

o   200g ground hazelnuts
o   600g buckwheat flour
o   350g ripe banana (mashed)
o   100ml maple syrup
o   100ml agave syrup
o   6 heaped tbsp coconut sugar
o   900ml almond milk
o   10 tbsp cacao powder
o   200 dates (pitted)
o   7 heaped tbsp tahini
o   3 heaped tbsp coconut oil

METHOD:

1.   Add your mashed banana, 450ml of your almond milk, 6 tbsp of your cacao powder, maple syrup, agave syrup, and coconut sugar to a blender and blend until smooth.

2.   Pour this mixture into a large bowl and add your buckwheat flour and ground hazelnuts, mixing well.

3.   Divide your cake mix into 2 lined cake tins- equally distributed.

4.   Bake your cakes in a preheated oven at 200c (or 180c if your oven runs hot) for approximately 25 minutes.

5.   Whilst the cakes are baking, start making your icing by adding your remaining almond milk and dates to a saucepan and heating on a medium heat.

6.   Constantly stir your mixture for around 20 minutes and ensure all the dates have broken down and softened with the milk changing colour slightly.

7.   Add your remaining cacao powder, coconut oil, and tahini stirring through on the heat for a couple of minutes. Remove from the heat and allow to cool.

8.   Once cooled, pour your icing mixture into your blender, blend until smooth, and set aside to decorate your cake later.

9.   Once your cakes are baked, remove from the oven and allow to cool.

10. Once cooled, decorate your cake by spreading half your icing on top of one cake and placing your second cake on top. Spread the remaining icing on top of your cake.

SUBSTITUTIONS:

If you don't have any buckwheat flour- you can use rice flour instead.

CHOCOLATE AND ALMOND ROCKS!

- Serving size: 8
- Difficulty: Easy
- Time: 30 minutes

INGREDIENTS:
o 200g ground almonds
o 100g buckwheat flour
o 50ml maple syrup
o 3 dates (pitted)
o 2 tbsp cacao powder
o 2 tbsp coconut oil
o 40ml water

METHOD:
1. Blend all the ingredients together to form a cookie dough.
2. Divide the mixture into eight, and roll each section into balls to form the rock shape.
3. Place your rocks onto a lined baking tray and bake in a preheated oven at 200c (or 180c if your oven runs hot!)
4. Allow the rocks to cool slightly and enjoy!

TOP TIP:
When placing your rocks on the baking tray- ensure there is enough space between the rocks to prevent them sticking together!

BUCKWHEAT, BANANA, AND APPLE MUFFINS

- Serving size: 12 muffins
- Difficulty: Moderate
- Time: 30 minutes

INGREDIENTS:
o   3 ripe bananas (mashed)
o   1 apple (cored and diced)
o   75ml coconut milk
o   1 tbsp vanilla extract
o   3 and a half tbsp coconut oil (melted)
o   230g buckwheat flour
o   200g coconut sugar
o   1 tsp bicarbonate soda
o   1 tsp baking powder
o   1 tsp ground cinnamon

METHOD:
1.   In a small bowl, mix together the mashed banana, milk, vanilla extract, and melted oil. Set aside.
2.   In a large bowl, mix together the flour, coconut sugar, bicarbonate of soda, baking powder, and cinnamon.
3.   Add the mashed banana mix into your dry ingredients and mix well.
4.   Add your chopped apple to the cake mix and mix well.
5.   Evenly distribute your cake mix into 12 cupcake cases on a muffin tray.
6.   Bake in a pre-heated oven at 180c (or 200c if your oven runs hot) for 25 minutes.
7.   Once baked, allow to cool before enjoying!

TOP TIP:
Try adding 100g of juicy sultanas to your mix at step 4 for an even fruitier taste!

BLUEBERRY AND STRAWBERRY SCONES

- Serving size: 12
- Difficulty: Moderate
- Time: 45 minutes

INGREDIENTS:
- o   380g rice/ buckwheat flour
- o   260g ground almonds
- o   300ml coconut milk
- o   4 tbsp maple syrup
- o   1 tbsp vanilla extract
- o   3 tbsp pureed apple
- o   225g strawberries (chopped)
- o   125g blueberries

METHOD:
1.   In a large bowl, mix together the flour, ground almonds, milk, maple syrup, vanilla extract, and pureed apple until smooth.
2.   Stir in the blueberries and chopped strawberries, ensuring they are evenly spread into the mixture.
3.   Divide the mixture into 12 sections and roll each section into a ball to form a scone shape.
4.   On 2 lined baking trays, place your scones evenly distanced apart and bake in a preheated oven at 180c (or 160c if your oven runs hot) for approximately 35-40 minutes.
5.   Once the scones are golden brown, remove the scones from the oven and allow to cool before serving.

TOP TIP:
You can top your scone with a splash of coconut cream (or the thick topping of coconut milk) to serve for a fresh treat!

SUBSTITUTION:
You can replace coconut milk with almond milk if you prefer the taste.

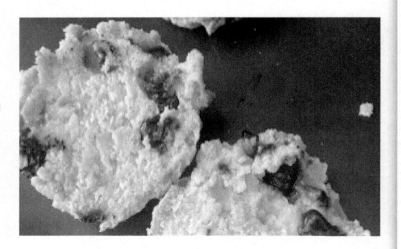

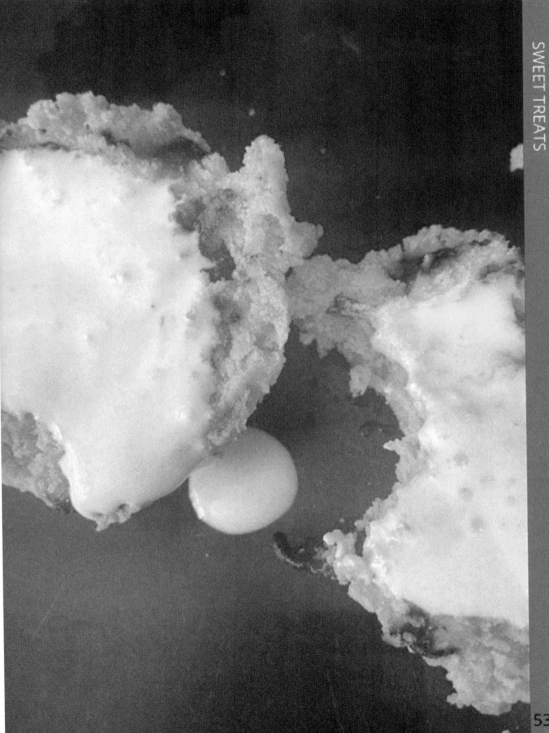

PEANUTTY POPCORN

- Serving size: 1 sharing bowl
- Difficulty: Easy
- Time: 15 minutes

INGREDIENTS:
o   200g popping corn kernels
o   6 tbsp coconut oil (melted)
o   4 tbsp peanut butter (melted)
o   1 and a half tbsp maple syrup
o   1 and a half tbsp coconut sugar

METHOD:
1.   Add half your coconut oil and all your corn kernels to a pan on a high heat and stir through. Ensure the lid is on as you watch your corn pop!
2.   Once all the corn has popped, remove from the heat and place the corn into a large bowl.
3.   In a pan on a medium heat, add your melted peanut butter and remaining coconut oil and mix well until combined.
4.   Gently stir in the coconut sugar and maple syrup. Keep stirring the mix to ensure it doesn't burn.
5.   Once all combined, pour the lix over your popcorn and mix well to ensure the popcorn is fully coated.

TOP TIP:
Keep shaking your pan as your corn is popping to prevent the corn burning or sticking to the bottom!

SUBSTITUTIONS:
You can use almond butter rather than peanut butter if you prefer the almondy flavour!

WHITE CHOCOLATE AND BERRY FLAPJACKS

INGREDIENTS:
o   150g jumbo oats
o   150g oat flour
o   4 tbsp maple/ agave syrup
o   200g dairy-free white chocolate chips
o   150g chopped fresh berries of your choice (I use 50g raspberries and 100g cherries)
o   100g coconut oil
o   75g peanut butter
o   2-3 tbsp of oat/almond milk

METHOD:
1.   Mix together the oats and oat flour in a large bowl and set aside.
2.   In a separate bowl, melt the peanut butter, coconut oil and maple/agave syrup together and leave to cool.
3.   Add the melted mixture to the oat mixture and mix until it begins to combine.
4.   Mix in your berries and 100g of your white chocolate chips until evenly distributed into the mix.
5.   Gently add your milk to the mixture one tbsp at a time until the mixture combines.
6.   Once combined, place the mixture into your lined baking tray ensuring it is evenly distributed across the tray.
7.   Cook in a preheated oven at 170c (if your oven runs hot cook at 160c) for approximately 15-17 minutes.
8.   Allow the mixture to cool before melting the remaining white chocolate chips and drizzling on the top!

TOP TIP:
You can blend regular oats to make your own oat flour!
Dairy free white chocolate can be found in most supermarkets and health stores.

SUBSTITUTIONS:
If you want to add some extra protein- substitute half your ground oats for 75g unflavoured/ vanilla protein powder.

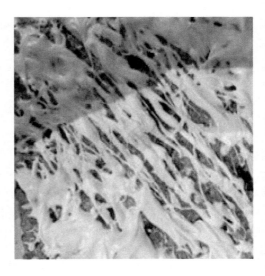

SEEDY AND STICKY GRANOLA BARS

- Serving size: Approximately 20 (1 large baking tray)
- Difficulty: Moderate
- Time: 45 minutes

INGREDIENTS:
o 20 pitted dates + 600ml water
o 250g sunflower seeds
o 250g pumpkin seeds
o 225g sultanas
o 265g oats
o 3 heaped tbsp chai seeds
o 2 tbsp cinnamon

METHOD:
1. In a large bowl, mix together your sunflower seeds, pumpkin seeds, sultanas, and oats and set aside.
2. Boil your dates in approximately 600ml water and simmer until the dates soften.
3. Once soft (after 5 minutes approximately) add the date mixture (including the water) to a blender with the chia seeds and cinnamon, and blend until smooth.
4. Add the date mixture to the oat mixture and mix well, coating all the ingredients.
5. Pour your mixture into a lined baking tray and ensure the mixture is evenly disturbed across the tray.
6. Bake in a preheated oven at 180c (or 160c if your oven runs hot) for approximately 30-40 minutes.
7. Allow to cool slightly before serving.

TOP TIPS:
Medjool dates are my favourite date to use and offer a great flavour and texture!

To help with cutting your mixture into bars- you can take your bake out the oven halfway through cooking, cut them into bars and place back in the oven for the remaining cooking time!

DARK CHOCOLATE AND CARAMEL NOUGAT BARS

- Serving size: 10
- Difficulty: Advanced
- Time: 1 hour 10 minutes (approximately)

INGREDIENTS:

o   140g cacao peanut butter (melted)
o   145ml maple syrup
o   3 tsp vanilla extract
o   40g ground almonds
o   185g dates (pitted)
o   1 tbsp tahini
o   4 tbsp coconut sugar
o   95g cacao liquor buttons

METHOD:

1.   On a low-medium heat, combine 50ml maple syrup with the melted cacao peanut butter, and heat until smooth.
2.   Remove from the heat and add the ground almonds, 1tsp vanilla extract, and mix well to form a dough.
3.   Press this dough evenly into a lined loaf tin before putting in the freezer for 15 minutes.
4.   Meanwhile, add the dates, tahini, 20ml maple syrup, and 1 tsp of vanilla extract to a blender and blend until smooth.
5.   Once 15 minutes has passed, remove the dough from the freezer and evenly spread the caramel on top of the dough to form the caramel layer. Place back in the freezer for another 15 minutes.
6.   Meanwhile, gently melt the cacao liquor buttons with the remaining maple syrup, vanilla extract, and coconut sugar- frequently stirring to ensure the sugar doesn't burn. Remove from the heat and set aside.
7.   Once 15 minutes has passed, remove the loaf tin from the freezer and cut into 10 slices.
8.   Dip each nougat bar into the melted chocolate and coat fully.
9.   Once all nougat bars are coated, place them on a baking tray and refrigerate for approximately 30 minutes before enjoying.

TOP TIP:

It is essential that the maple syrup and coconut sugar is not left out when making the chocolate topping as cacao liquor buttons are very bitter on their own.

SUBSTITUTIONS:

If you don't have any cacao peanut butter, you can substitute this for regular peanut butter for a less chocolatey taste!

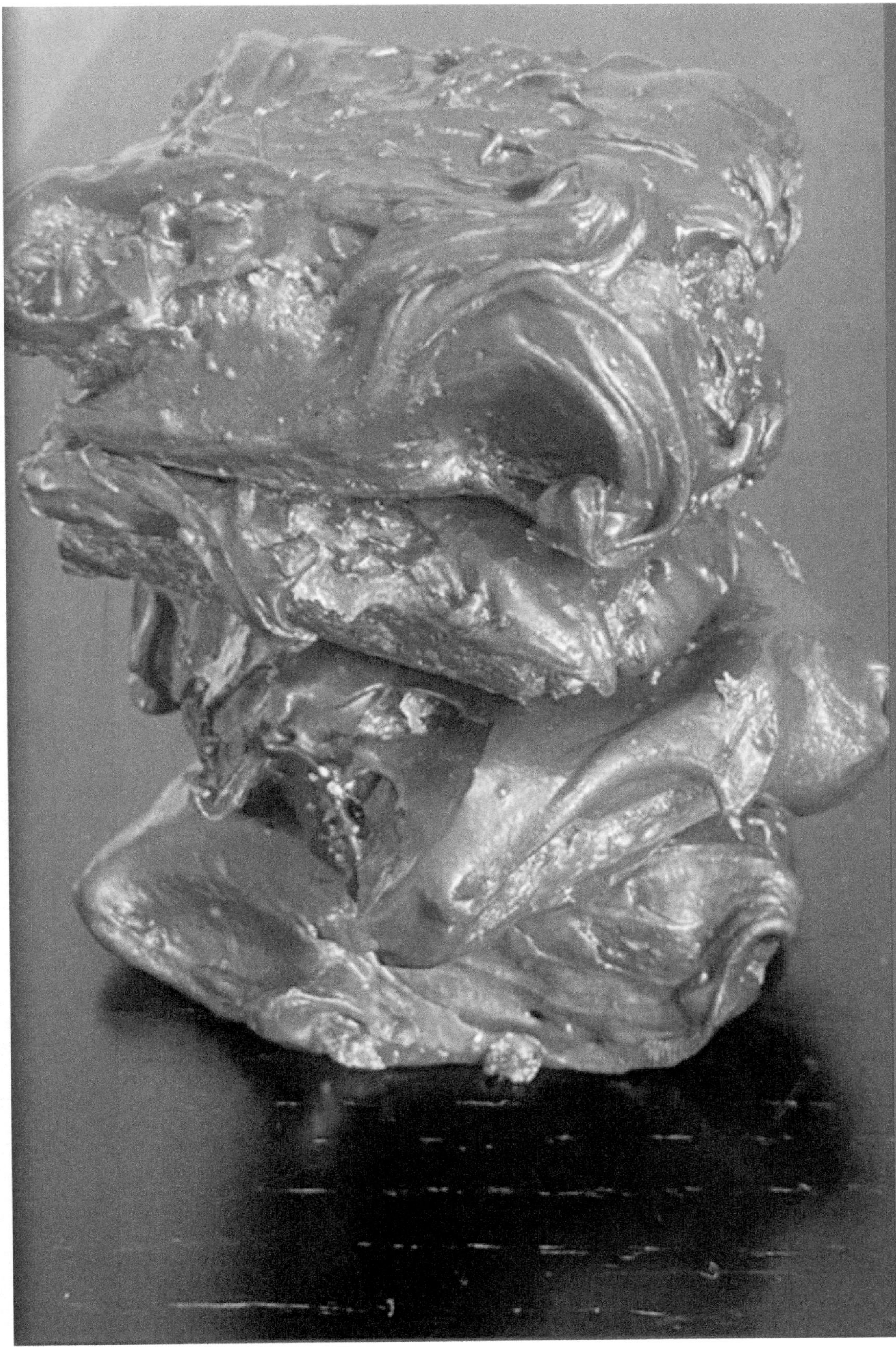

CHOCOLATE PROTEIN ICE-CREAM BARS

- Serving size: 16 bars (approx)
- Difficulty: Easy
- Time: 10 minutes (plus 2 hours 30 minutes freeze time!)

INGREDIENTS:
- o   150g natural chocolate protein powder
- o   2 tbsp cacao powder
- o   30g ground almonds
- o   80g hazelnut butter
- o   80ml maple syrup
- o   250ml water
- o   2 tsp coconut oil (melted)
- o   180g natural vegan chocolate (chopped)

METHOD:
1.   In a blender, blend all the ingredients together- except the coconut oil and vegan chocolate.
2.   Once smooth, pour the mixture into a lined loaf tin and place in the freezer for 2 hours.
3.   After the mixture has set, melt the coconut oil and chocolate together in a separate bowl.
4.   Once melted, pour over the set frozen mixture and place back in the freezer for 30 minutes.
5.   Cut into bars and enjoy!

TOP TIP:
Keep these bars in the freezer as they will melt in the fridge!

SUBSTITUTIONS:
If you don't have any natural chocolate protein powder, you can use 125g natural unflavoured protein powder mixed with an additional 25g of cacao powder.

If you don't have enough maple syrup, you can substitute half the maple syrup for agave syrup.

NO-CHURN EASY PEANUT BUTTER ICE-CREAM

- Serving size: 1 tub
- Difficulty: Easy
- Time: 5 minutes (+12 hours freezing)

INGREDIENTS:
o   350ml oat milk
o   250g peanut butter
o   11 pitted dates

METHOD:
1.   Blend all the ingredients together in a strong blender until smooth.
2.   Place the mixture into a freezer-proof container and freeze for 12 hours (or overnight).
3.   Once frozen, remove at least ten minutes before serving to ensure a creamy texture.

TOP TIP:
Sometimes the ice cream can become quite solid in the freezer. If that happens, just ensure you take it out of the freezer half an hour before serving to ensure it melts slightly. Do not microwave it!

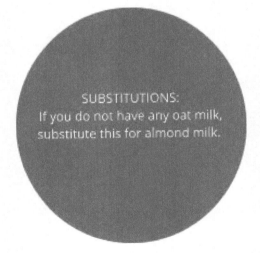

SUBSTITUTIONS:
If you do not have any oat milk, substitute this for almond milk.

NO-CHURN BANANA AND PECAN NICE-CREAM

- Serving size: 1 tub
- Difficulty: Easy
- Time: 10 minutes (+3 hours freezing)

INGREDIENTS:
o   2 bananas (sliced and frozen)
o   200ml coconut milk (and an extra splash!)
o   50ml coconut cream
o   70g chopped pecans
o   100g coconut sugar
o   1 tbsp cinnamon (optional)

METHOD:
1.   On a very low heat, warm the coconut sugar in a pan with the splash of coconut milk and stir constantly to form a thick liquid.
2.   When the liquid begins to boil, add your chopped pecans and remove from the heat.
3.   Stir the mixture and set aside to cool.
4.   Add your bananas, coconut milk, coconut cream and cinnamon (if using) to your blender and blend until a smooth consistency- no lumps!
5.   Remove the mixture from the blender and fill your tub ready to freeze.
6.   Gently swirl in your pecan mix to the desired consistency.
7.   Freeze for approximately 3 hours (or more if able) to form a solid ice cream texture.
8.   Serve and enjoy!

TOP TIPS:
Sometimes the nice cream can become quite solid in the freezer. If that happens, just ensure you take it out of the freezer half an hour before serving to ensure it melts slightly. Do not microwave the nice cream!

I love serving this with a spoonful of hazelnut butter or cacao chocolate spread!

CHOCOLATE CHIP AND GRANOLA ICE-CREAM

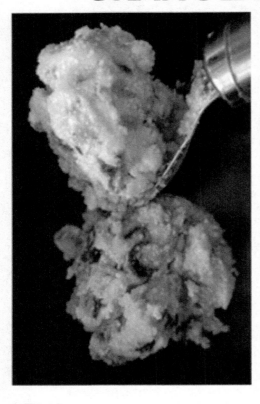

- Serving size: 1 medium tub
- Difficulty: Advanced
- Time: 20 minutes (plus 1 hour chilling and 6 hours freezing!)

INGREDIENTS:
o   400ml coconut milk (tinned)
o   60g unrefined caster cane sugar
o   70ml agave nectar
o   75g granola
o   85g semi-sweet dairy-free chocolate chips

TOP TIPS:
Take out your ice cream out of the freezer 5-10 minutes before eating to ensure it is of an appropriate consistency to scoop!

Ensure your ice-cream maker is pre-prepared before starting the recipe by placing the ice cream bowl in the freezer 12 hours in advance or as per the manufacturer's instructions.

METHOD:
1.   Blend together all the ingredients except the granola and chocolate chips.
2.   Place this mixture into an air-tight container and chill in the fridge for at least one hour.
3.   Once chilled, add the mix to the pre-prepared ice cream maker and churn as per manufacturer's instructions. Churn for approximately 10-15 minutes until a soft-serve consistency is achieved.
4.   Place the soft-serve ice-cream mix into a freezer safe air-tight container and fold in the granola and chocolate chips.
5.   Smooth the top of the ice-cream, cover, and place in the freezer for 6 hours or until firm.

SUBSTITUTIONS:
Why not use my fruit and nut protein granola recipe for a nutty protein twist?

RICH COOKIE-DOUGH SLUSH!

- Serving size: 1 small tub
- Difficulty: Advanced
- Time: 30 minutes (plus 1 hour chilling and 6 hours freezing!)

INGREDIENTS:

FOR THE COOKIE DOUGH:
o   1 tbsp coconut oil (melted)
o   1 tbsp coconut sugar
o   Half a tsp vanilla extract
o   15g rice flour
o   1 and a half tbsp soya protein powder
o   1 and a half tbsp soya milk

FOR THE ICE-CREAM:
o   320ml coconut milk (from a carton)
o   35g coconut sugar
o   1 and a half tbsp agave nectar
o   1 tbsp vanilla extract
o   2 tbsp dairy-free milk chocolate (chopped)

Method:
1.   To make the ice-cream, blend together the coconut milk, coconut sugar, agave nectar, and vanilla extract and place in an air-tight container to chill in the fridge for one hour.
2.   Meanwhile, make the cookie dough by spreading the rice flour on a line baking tray and bake in a preheated oven at 175c for approximately 5 minutes. Cool before continuing.
3.   Blend together the coconut oil, coconut sugar, and vanilla extract and place in a bowl.
4.   Add the cool rice flour, soya protein and soya milk to the bowl and mix together well to form the cookie dough. Split into small sized balls before setting aside.
5.   Once the ice-cream mix has chilled, add it to the pre-prepared ice cream maker and churn as per manufacturer's instructions. Churn for approximately 10-15 minutes until a soft-serve consistency is achieved.
6.   Place the soft-serve ice-cream mix into a freezer safe air-tight container and fold in the cookie-dough balls and chopped chocolate.
7.   Smooth the top of the ice-cream, cover, and place in the freezer for 6 hours or until firm.

TOP TIP:
Ensure your ice-cream maker is pre-prepared before starting the recipe by placing the ice cream bowl in the freezer 12 hours in advance or as per the manufacturer's instructions.

SUBSTITUTIONS:
For a less slushy snow cone texture- use coconut milk that is from a tin as opposed to a carton.

65

SWEET PISTACHIO NIBBLES

- Serving size: 1 bowl
- Difficulty: Moderate
- Time: 15 minutes

INGREDIENTS:
o 200g coconut sugar
o 240ml water
o 50g chopped pistachio kernels
o 1 tbsp almond extract

TOP TIPS:
This recipe is easier if you can find pistachio kernels that are already roasted! If you can, skip the first step.

Ensure you frequently stir your sugar and water mix to prevent the sugar burning!

METHOD:
1. Place your chopped pistachio kernels on a lined baking tray and bake in a preheated oven at 180c for 8 minutes until roasted. Once roasted, remove from the oven and set aside.
2. Add your sugar and water to a saucepan on a low-medium heat and bring to the boil. Once boiling, reduce the heat and allow to simmer for 5 minutes- stirring occasionally.
3. Add your roasted chopped pistachios to the syrup mixture and allow it to simmer for 5-10 minutes whilst frequently stirring.
4. Remove from the heat and stir in the almond extract.
5. Using a sieve, pour your syrup mixture into a bowl over the sieve catching all the pistachio kernels into the sieve. Set the syrup aside.
6. Add your pistachio nibbles to a bowl and enjoy!

· ·

- Serving size: 1 bowl
- Difficulty: Easy
- Time: 15 minutes

CANDIED PECAN

NIBBLES

INGREDIENTS:
o 100g pecans (chopped)
o 45ml maple syrup

METHOD:
1. Mix together your pecans and maple syrup- ensure all the nuts are coated.
2. Scatter the pecans onto a lined baking tray- ensuring none are on top of each-other.
3. Bake in a preheated oven at 180c for 7 minutes approx.
4. Remove the pecans from the oven and mix through to ensure all sides of the pecans can be toasted.
5. Place bake in the oven for a further 3-7 minutes dependent on your level of toasted preference.

TOP TIP:
I prefer to cut my pecans into quarters- but you can keep them bigger or chop them up more dependent on your preference.

Snacks, sides, and sauces

PAPRIKA AND PEA BREAD

- Serving size: 1 loaf
- Difficulty: Moderate
- Time: 1 hour 15 minutes

INGREDIENTS:
o   30g ground flaxseed (+ 6 tbsp water)
o   350g buckwheat flour
o   50g oats
o   1 and half tsp baking powder
o   1 and half tsp bicarbonate of soda
o   2 and a half tbsp smoked paprika
o   2 tsp cumin
o   2 and half tsp ground coriander
o   1 and a half tbsp nutritional yeast
o   320ml oat milk
o   100ml olive oil
o   400g peas

TOP TIP:
I love drizzling some cold dairy free/
organic yoghurt over the warm bread
for a unique full flavour!

METHOD:
1.   Mix together the ground flax seeds with the water and set aside. Allow the mixture to combine for ten minutes.
2.   In a large bowl, combine the buckwheat flour, oats, baking powder, bicarbonate of soda, paprika, cumin, ground coriander and nutritional yeast. Mix well until smooth.
3.   Add your flax seed mixture, oat milk, olive oil, and peas to the bowl and mix well.
4.   Add your mixture to a lined loaf tin and bake in a preheated oven at 180c (or 160c if your oven runs hot) for 1 hour.
5.   Allow to cool slightly before serving.

PUMPKIN AND SUNFLOWER ALMOND BREAD

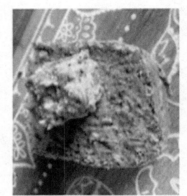

- Serving size: 1 loaf (approximately 20 slices)
- Difficulty: Moderate
- Time: 2 hours 20 mins

INGREDIENTS:
o   210g ground almonds
o   150g ground sunflower seeds
o   100g whole pumpkin seeds
o   200g rice flour (you can use buckwheat flour if you prefer)
o   3 heaped tbsp of psyllium husk powder
o   5 heaped tbsp of oregano
o   600ml cold water

METHOD:
1.   Mix all the ingredients in a large bowl, adding the water last to combine it all.
2.   Once a dough mixture has formed- gently cover the bowl with cling film and leave to rest for approximately 1 hour and 30 minutes.
3.   After this time has passed, place the mixture into a lined, average sized loaf tin (you shouldn't have any mixture left over).
4.   Bake the dough in a preheated oven at 200c (if your oven runs hot- bake at 180c) for 45 minutes.
5.   Ensure the bread is golden brown in colour and cooked in the inside before removing. (If you put a baking tool in the centre of the bread it should come out clean and not doughy or wet).
6.   Leave to cool slightly and enjoy!

TOP TIP:
You can use 210g of whole almonds and blend them yourself to make ground almonds if you prefer.

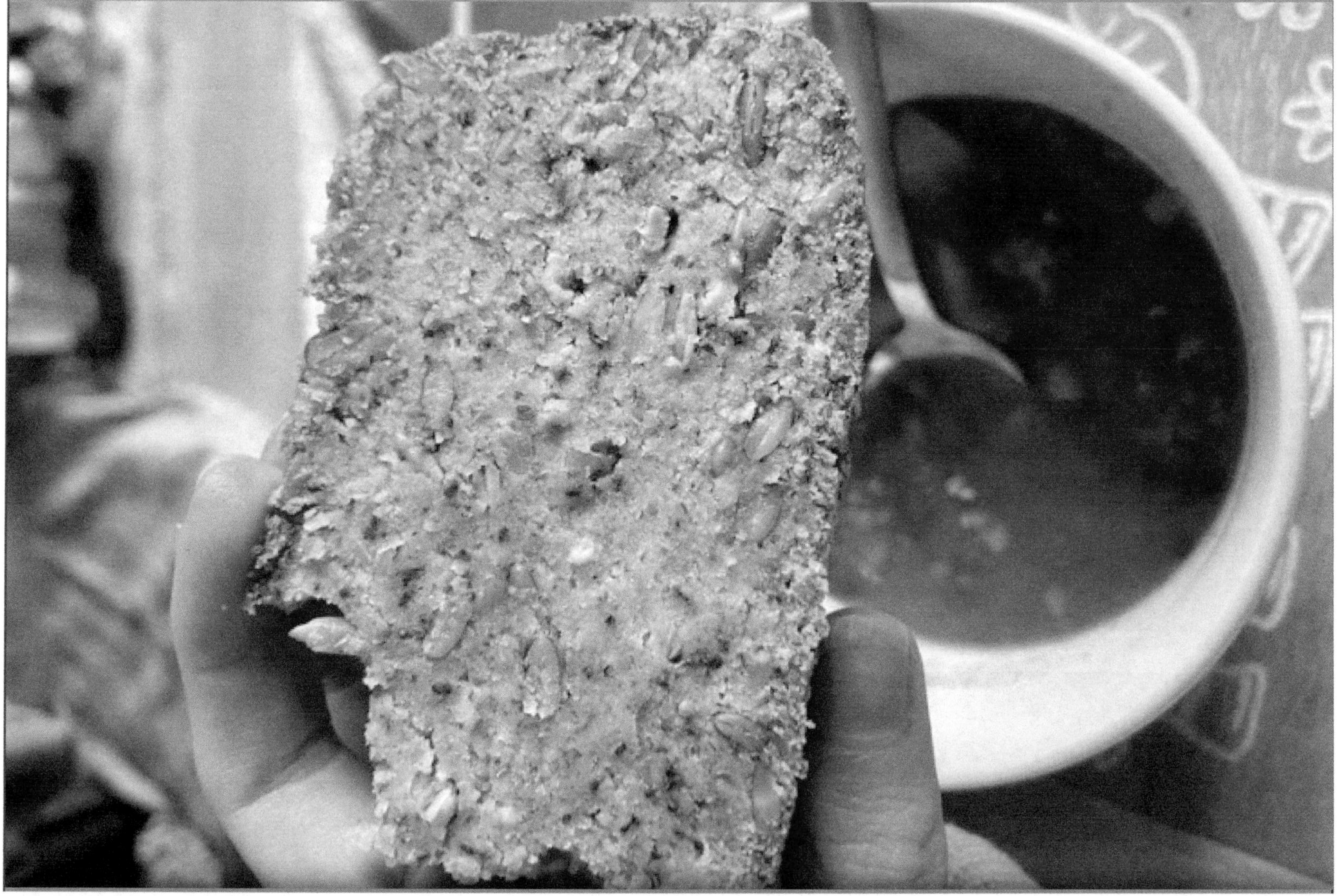

- Serving size: 1 loaf
- Difficulty: Advanced
- Time: 140 minutes

TOMATO AND BASIL FOCACCIA

INGREDIENTS:
o   A few splashes of olive oil
o   310ml warm water
o   40g natural yeast
o   500g natural bread flour (+ more for flouring)
o   1 tbsp oregano
o   150g sundried tomatoes in oil (chopped)
o   A few fresh basil leaves
o   Sprinkle of sea salt

METHOD:
1.   In a bowl, add the yeast to the warm water, stir well, and set aside for approximately 10 minutes.
2.   After 10 minutes, mix together your bread flour and oregano in a large bowl, and gently pour the yeast mixture into the bowl, stirring well.
3.   Stir in approximately 4 tbsp of the oil from your sundried tomatoes, and use your hands to form a dough.
4.   Flour a clean surface and knead the dough for approximately 10 minutes until smooth.
5.   Put your dough on a lined baking tray and cover with a tea towel. Allow the dough to prove for one hour and a half (longer if able) in a warm place.
6.   After the time has passed, knock the dough back on a clean (lightly floured) surface. You do this by punching the dough a few times to help mould the air bubbles formed in the dough to the shape you desire.
7.   Evenly spread your dough out onto your lined baking tray and gently poke multiple shallow holes into the bread.
8.   Scatter your sundried tomatoes, sea salt, and fresh basil on top of the dough- pushing some into the holes you have formed.
9.   Place your dough in a preheated oven at 200c (180c if your oven runs hot), and bake for approximately 20-30 minutes until golden.

TOP TIPS:
When you're kneading your dough- press the dough and if it bounces back and is smooth then it is ready for the next step.
When proofing your dough- your dough should have doubled in size before it is ready for the next step.

SUSTITUTIONS:
If you don't like the taste of basil, you can substitute it for fresh rosemary sprigs!

SEEDY CARROT CRACKERS!

- Serving size: 2
- Difficulty: Easy
- Time: 100 minutes

INGREDIENTS:
o   200g carrot (finely grated)
o   120g ground almonds
o   150g sunflower seeds
o   20g chia seeds
o   3 tbsp olive oil
o   1 tbsp tahini
o   1 tbsp tamari
o   Sprinkle of salt and pepper

TOP TIPS:
Ensure the mixture is sticky and pressed down to form a thin and compact mixture on the baking tray before placing in the oven.

Store these crackers in an airtight container at room temperature to ensure they do not go stale or soggy!

METHOD:
1.   In a large bowl, mix together all the ingredients.
2.   Add the mixture to a lined flat baking tray- spreading the mixture out evenly.
3.   Bake in a pre-heated oven at 110c (90c if your oven runs hot) for 90 minutes until golden and crispy!

SESAME-TOASTED POTATO CRISPS

- Serving size: 1 bowl
- Difficulty: Easy
- Time: 30 minutes

INGREDIENTS:
o   1 medium white potato (sliced)
o   3 tbsp sesame oil
o   Generous sprinkle of sea salt

METHOD:
1.   Add the sesame oil to a shallow bowl, and dip each potato slice in the sesame oil to fully coat before placing them onto a lined baking tray.
2.   Once all slices are coated, ensure that none of the slices are on top of each other and sprinkle them all with a generous portion of salt to taste.
3.   Bake in a preheated oven at 200c 10-15 minutes (dependent on the thickness of the slices-the thicker the slice, the longer it will need to crisp up).
4.   Remove from the oven and carefully turn each potato slice over to cook the other sides.
5.   Place the slices back in the oven for a further 10 minutes approximately until crisp around the edges and golden brown.

TOP TIPS:
Try to not peel your potatoes when slicing them, as I find the potato peel adds to the crispness and flavour.

Ensure you carefully watch the second time you bake your crisps as they will crisp up quicker than the first time in the oven!

MIXED-BEAN NUTTY POTATO SALAD

- Serving size: 4
- Difficulty: Moderate
- Time: 15 minutes

INGREDIENTS:
- 1kg cooked new potatoes
- 300g pre-soaked mixed beans
- 4 tbsp peanut butter
- 3 tsp tamari
- 3 tbsp sesame oil
- Juice of 1 lime
- 1 tbsp maple syrup
- 4 tbsp almond milk
- Handful of coriander
- Salt and pepper to season

METHOD:
1. In a small bowl, make the nutty sauce by mixing together the peanut butter, tamari, sesame oil, lime juice, maple syrup and almond milk, and set aside.
2. In a large bowl add you potatoes, mixed beans and coriander together.
3. Add your sauce to your potato and bean mixture, thoroughly coating the ingredients.
4. Season with salt and pepper before serving.

SUBSTITUTIONS:
If you don't have any pre-soaked beans, you can use a can of mixed beans that are pre-drained and rinsed.

SWEET POTATO AND BROCCOLI ROAST

- Serving size: 2
- Difficulty: Moderate
- Time: 40 minutes

INGREDIENTS:
o   1 large sweet potato (diced)
o   300g broccoli (chopped)
o   4 tbsp sesame oil
o   2 tbsp tamari
o   2 tbsp white miso paste
o   1 tbsp white rice vinegar
o   Juice of half a lemon
o   1 tbsp oregano
o   Sprinkle of garlic salt and pepper

TOP TIP:
Ensure the sweet potatoes and broccoli are fully coated in the sauce for a full flavour!

METHOD:
1.   In a small bowl, combine the miso paste, sesame oil, tamari, lemon juice, and white rice vinegar- mixing well.
2.   On a large, lined baking tray, scatter the diced sweet potato evenly spread onto the tray. Pour half of the sauce over the sweet potatoes, ensuring they are fully coated in the sauce.
3.   Bake the sweet potato in a preheated oven at 200c (or 220c if your oven runs hot) for 25 minutes.
4.   Meanwhile, marinate the broccoli pieces by adding them to the remaining sauce mixture and coating them thoroughly before setting aside.
5.   After the 25 minutes have passed, remove the tray from the oven and scatter across the marinated broccoli and oregano, mixing well with the sweet potato.
6.   Place the sweet potato and broccoli back in the oven for a further ten minutes.
7.   Once cooked, remove from the oven and sprinkle over the salt and pepper before serving.

SUBSTITUTIONS:
If you don't have any white miso paste or white rice vinegar, you can use brown miso paste or brown rice vinegar instead.

SIMPLE SIDE SALAD

- Serving size: 1 large bowl
- Difficulty: Easy
- Time: 5 minutes

INGREDIENTS:
o   Large handful of coriander (chopped)
o   400g sweetcorn
o   Half a cucumber (diced)
o   Half a red pepper (chopped)

METHOD:
Simply, mix all together and enjoy!

SUBSTITUTIONS:
The best part about both of these recipes is that they are so diverse! I always use the coriander as a base in my side salad (and the grapes in my fruit salad)- but often switch up the other ingredients for whatever I have in the fridge or fancy having that day!

- Serving size: 1 large bowl
- Difficulty: Easy
- Time: 5 minutes

INGREDIENTS:
o   punnet of grapes
o   Half a honeydew melon (chopped)
o   1 tin of peaches in juice (drained)

METHOD:
Simply, mix all together and enjoy!

SIMPLE FRUIT SALAD

TOP TIP:
Both of these salads are great to prep for the week ahead- making nutritious food easily accessible to accompany your week-night dishes or to have as a quick healthy snack!

YOGHURT AND MINT DIP

- Serving size: 4
- Difficulty: Easy
- Time: 5 minutes

INGREDIENTS:
o   75g natural dairy-free yoghurt
o   1 tbsp dried mint
o   Sprinkle of salt and pepper

METHOD:
Mix all together and enjoy!

GUACAMOLE

- Serving size: 4
- Difficulty: Easy
- Time: 5 minutes

INGREDIENTS:
o   1 large avocado
o   1 handful of coriander (chopped)
o   Juice of half a lime

METHOD:
Mash all together and enjoy!

PAPRIKA HUMMUS

- Serving size: 1 sharing bowl
- Difficulty: Easy
- Time: 5 minutes

Ingredients:
o   400g pre-soaked chickpeas (soft)
o   2 and a half tbsp tahini
o   Half a tsp cumin
o   2 tsp paprika (smoked if able)
o   Juice of half a lemon
o   Sprinkle of salt and pepper
o   Splash of water (as needed)

METHOD:
1.   Blend all ingredients together in a blender.
2.   If the mixture appears to be dry- gently add water until desired consistency is reached.
3.   Scoop the mixture into a bowl and serve.

TOP TIP:
I really enjoy this as a dip for my sesame-toasted potato crisps or an accompany to any of my pasta dishes!

Smoothies, shots, and other drinks

GREEN FEEL-GOOD SMOOTHIE

- Serving size: 1
- Difficulty: Easy
- Time: 5 minutes

INGREDIENTS:
o   Half medium banana (frozen or ripe)
o   2 tbsp oats
o   Handful of ice
o   Handful of spinach (fresh or frozen)
o   1 tbsp spirulina powder
o   1 tbsp peanut butter
o   1 and a half tbsp maple or agave syrup
o   100ml rice-milk
o   Half thumb sized piece of fresh ginger finely chopped (optional)
o   1 tbsp of chia seeds (optional)
o   1 tbsp unflavoured or vanilla soy/pea/hemp protein powder (optional)

METHOD:
Blend all together and enjoy!

SUBSTITUTIONS:
You can use almond milk rather than rice milk for a less sweet taste if preferred.

82

PINK PASSION SMOOTHIE

- Serving size: 1
- Difficulty: Easy
- Time: 5 minutes

INGREDIENTS:
o   Half a dragon-fruit (chopped)
o   Handful of mixed berries (I use blueberries and raspberries)
o   50g coconut/dairy free yoghurt
o   Handful of ice
o   100ml coconut/rice milk
o   2 tbsp maple syrup

METHOD:
Blend all together and enjoy!

TOP TIP:
Dragon fruit can often taste un-sweet or bland- therefore I prefer to add 2 tbsp of maple syrup instead of one. But feel free to half the maple syrup if you want a less sweet smoothie.

SUBSTITUTIONS:
You can replace the coconut/rice milk with almond milk for a less sweet taste.

RED BERRY SMOOTHIE

- Serving size: 1
- Difficulty: Easy
- Time: 5 minutes

INGREDIENTS:
o Half medium banana (frozen or ripe)
o 80g frozen mixed berries (I use 40g raspberries and 40g strawberries)
o 50ml cold water/Handful of ice
o Large spoonful of dairy-free natural yoghurt (the more you use, the thicker your smoothie!)
o 1 tbsp almond butter
o 1 and a half tbsp maple or agave syrup
o 1 tsp maca or acai berry powder (optional)

METHOD:
Blend all together and enjoy!

SUBSTITUTIONS:
You can use peanut butter or hazelnut butter if you prefer a stronger nutty flavour!

PURPLE PROTEIN-POWER SMOOTHIE

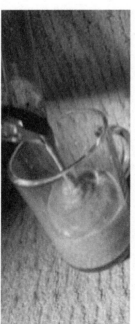

- Serving size: 2
- Difficulty: Easy
- Time: 5 minutes

METHOD:
Blend all together and enjoy!

INGREDIENTS:
o 160g blueberries (frozen or fresh)
o 1 medium banana (frozen or ripe)
o 2 tbsp soy/pea/hemp protein powder (unflavoured)
o Approx 8 cubes of ice
o 2 tbsp of chia seeds
o 6 pitted dates
o 2 tsp maple syrup
o 100ml pressed blueberry juice (optional)

TOP TIP:
If you prefer a thicker consistency- leave out the blueberry juice. However, I think it adds a great natural sweetness and flavour!

SUBSTITUTIONS:
If you don't have any chai seeds- feel free to substitute this with linseeds or flaxseeds.
If you prefer some flavour to your protein powder- I would suggest a neutral flavour for example vanilla or blueberry for taste.

PRUNE AND BLUEBERRY BREAKFAST JUICE

- Serving size: 1
- Difficulty: Easy
- Time: 5 minutes

INGREDIENTS:
- o 230ml pure prune juice
- o 80g blueberries (frozen or fresh)
- o 100g dairy free yoghurt
- o Approx 4 cubes of ice
- o 1 tbsp maple syrup

METHOD:
Blend all together and enjoy!

TOP TIPS:
If you prefer a less thick consistency- leave out the yoghurt. However, I think it adds a creamier taste and texture!

For an additional protein kick- add 1 tbsp unflavoured soy/pea/hemp protein powder.

- -

HERB JUICE!

- Serving size:1
- Difficulty: Easy
- Time: 5 minutes

INGREDIENTS:
- o 1 green apple
- o Half a cucumber
- o 2 celery sticks
- o Small handful of parsley (chopped)
- o Small handful of mint (chopped)
- o Small handful of coriander
- o 1 tsp agave nectar

METHOD:
1. Use a juicer to juice all the ingredients together except the agave nectar.
2. Once juiced, mix in a glass with the agave nectar and enjoy!

PURE GREEN PLANT JUICE

- Serving size: 2
- Difficulty: Easy
- Time: 5 minutes

INGREDIENTS:
- 1 green apple
- 1 cucumber
- Handful of spinach
- 3 celery stalks
- 60g broccoli
- 2tsp agave nectar

METHOD:
1. Use a juicer to juice all the ingredients together except the agave nectar.
2. Once juiced, mix in a glass with the agave nectar and enjoy!

PURE RED PLANT JUICE

- Serving size: 1
- Difficulty: Easy
- Time: 5 minutes

INGREDIENTS:
- 1 small beetroot
- 2 medium carrots
- 1 thumb sized piece of ginger root (peeled)
- I orange (peeled)
- Juice of half lemon
- 1tsp agave nectar

METHOD:
1. Use a juicer to juice all the ingredients together except the agave nectar.
2. Once juiced, mix in a glass with the agave nectar and enjoy!

APPLE AND MANGO GINGER-SHOTS

- Serving size: 6 shots
- Difficulty: Easy
- Time: 5 minutes

INGREDIENTS:
- o 250ml pure apple and mango juice
- o 100ml pure apple cider vinegar
- o 1 heaped tbsp of fresh ginger (finely grated)
- o Half tsp turmeric (optional)

METHOD:
Blend all together and serve into 6 shot glasses or containers!

SUBSTITUTIONS:
You can use just pure apple or mango juice instead of a combination of both if your prefer.

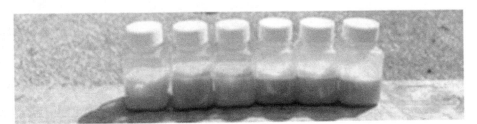

ADRENAL SUPPORT SHOTS

- Serving size: 6 shots
- Difficulty: Easy
- Time: 5 minutes

INGREDIENTS:
- o 125ml pure pineapple juice
- o 125ml pure coconut water
- o 100ml apple cider vinegar
- o Sprinkle of salt

TOP TIP:
This drink is to help aid function of the adrenal glands and is often taken in the afternoon to help prevent the 'afternoon slump'. However, this is not to serve as a substitute for medical care, advice, and support. Please seek medical and professional advice as needed.

METHOD:
1. Blend together and split into 6 shots to enjoy!

Substitution:
You can replace pineapple juice for pure orange juice if you prefer- an additional source of vitamin C!

MANGO-COLADA SLUSHIE COCKTAIL!

- Serving size:2
- Difficulty: Easy
- Time: 5 minutes

INGREDIENTS:
o 110ml pure mango puree
o 40ml coconut rum
o 2 handfuls of ice

METHOD:
Blend all together and enjoy!

SUBSTITUTIONS;
For an alcohol-free version, replace the coconut rum with coconut water.

• •

GINGERBREAD ICED LATTE

- Serving size: 2
- Difficulty: Easy
- Time: 5 minutes

INGREDIENTS:
o 250ml rice-milk
o 1 tbsp natural gingerbread syrup
o Half tsp fresh ginger (finely chopped)
o A shot of espresso
o Handful of ice

METHOD:
Blend all together and enjoy!

SUBSTITUTIONS:
If you don't have any rice milk, you can substitute this for almond milk or oat milk. However, the rice-milk really adds to the sweet flavour!

PISTACHIO AND ALMOND SYRUP

- Serving size: 1 jar
- Difficulty: Moderate
- Time: 15 minutes

INGREDIENTS:
o   200g coconut sugar
o   240ml water
o   50g chopped pistachio kernels
o   1 tbsp almond extract

METHOD::
1.   Place your chopped pistachio kernels on a lined baking tray and bake in a preheated oven at 180c for 8 minutes until roasted. Once roasted, remove from the oven and set aside.
2.   Add your sugar and water to a saucepan on a low-medium heat and bring to the boil. Once boiling, reduce the heat and allow to simmer for 5 minutes-stirring occasionally.
3.   Add your roasted chopped pistachios to the syrup mixture and allow it to simmer for 5-10 minutes whilst frequently stirring.
4.   Remove from the heat and stir in the almond extract.
5.   Using a sieve, pour your syrup mixture into a bowl over the sieve catching all the pistachio kernels into the sieve. Set the pistachios aside.
6.   Pour your syrup into an airtight jar or container to use when desired.

TOP TIPS:
Try adding the pistachio syrup to iced lattes or drizzling over a yoghurt breakfast bowl for a sweet addition!

SWEET PISTACHIO LATTE

- Serving size: 1 latte (+ 1 jar of syrup and 1 bowl of pistachio nibbles!)
- Difficulty: Moderate
- Time: 20 minutes

INGREDIENTS:
o   200g coconut sugar
o   240ml water
o   50g chopped pistachio kernels
o   1 tbsp almond extract
o   200ml rice-milk
o   1 espresso

METHOD:
1.   Place your chopped pistachio kernels on a lined baking tray and bake in a preheated oven at 180c for 8 minutes until roasted. Once roasted, remove from the oven and set aside.
2.   Add your sugar and water to a saucepan on a low-medium heat and bring to the boil. Once boiling, reduce the heat and allow to simmer for 5 minutes- stirring occasionally.
3.   Add your roasted chopped pistachios to the syrup mixture and allow it to simmer for 5-10 minutes whilst frequently stirring.
4.   Remove from the heat and stir in the almond extract.
5.   Using a sieve, pour your syrup mixture into a bowl over the sieve catching all the pistachio kernels into the sieve. Set the pistachios aside to eat when desired.
6.   Pour your syrup into an airtight jar or container and set aside.
7.   Heat up your milk to your desired temperature and pour into your glass/mug with your espresso and 3 heaped tsp's of your syrup.
8.   Mix well and top with a few pistachio nibbles before enjoying!

TOP TIP:
Keep the pistachio nibbles for a delicious snack!
Substitutions:
If you don't have any rice milk, you can substitute this for a milk of your choice, but it may not be as sweet.

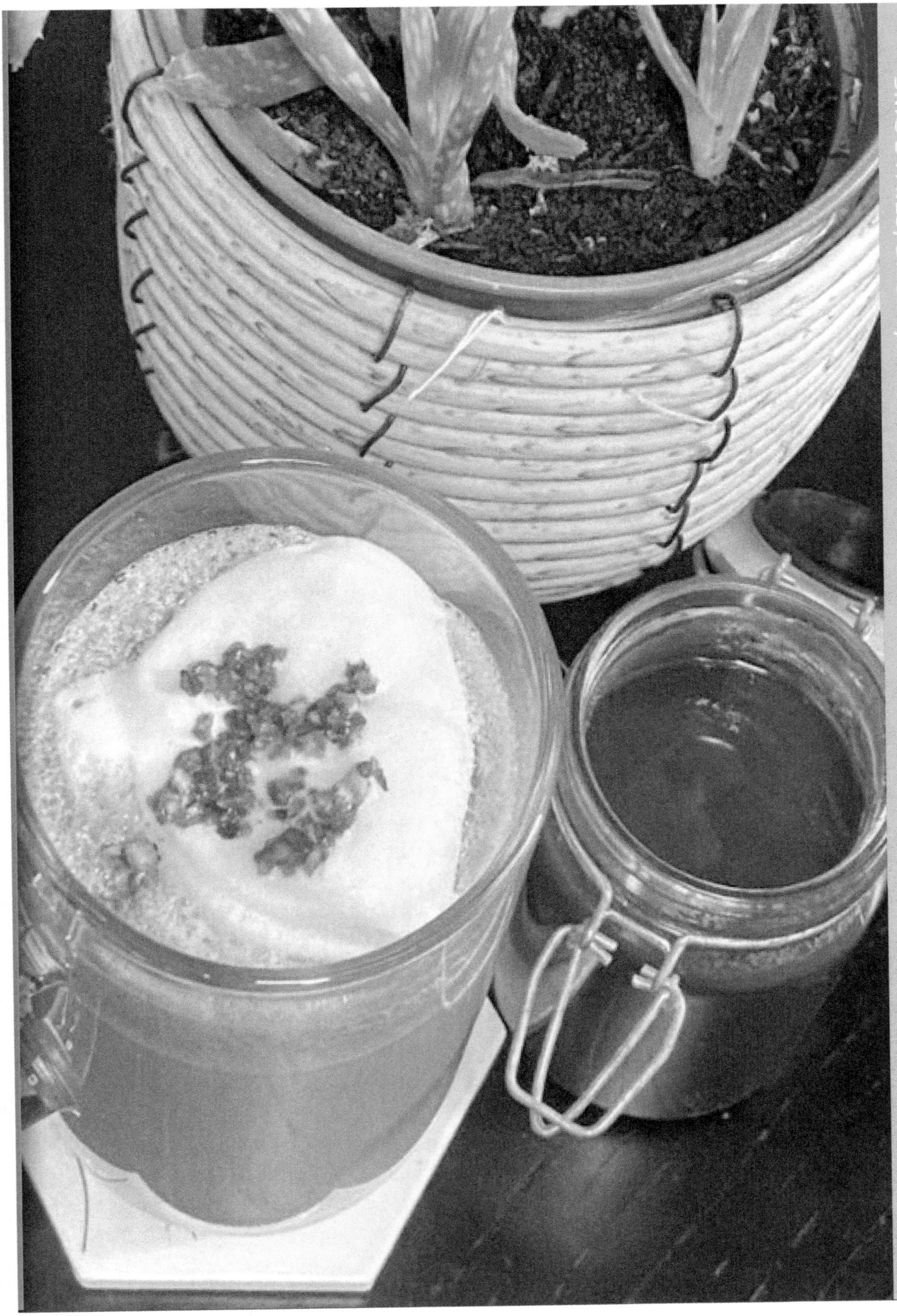

Index

Definitions

Anorexia Nervosa: A diagnosed eating disorder that is recognised as a mental health condition where one is typically presented as low in body weight and preoccupied with food/ body image.

Anxiety: Intense feeling of worry/fear/unease which can present with various additional physical and mental health symptoms.

Bulimia Nervosa: A diagnosed eating disorder that is recognised as a mental health condition where one regularly consumes large quantities of food to then purge/ fast afterwards, with a preoccupation around food/ body image.

Depression: Intense feeling of sadness/despair/low mood which can present with various additional physical and mental health symptoms.

Cortisol: The stress hormone that is released to help your body regulate.

Covid 19: A contagious virus primarily affecting the respiratory system.

Clean or clean eating: Foods that are natural with no added chemicals or preservatives.

Healthy: Feeling good physically, emotionally, mentally, and spiritually with long term sustainability in accordance with your unique needs and accessibility.

Irritable Bowel Syndrome: A diagnosed syndrome that effects the digestive system.

Myalgic Encephalomyelitis/ Chronic Fatigue Syndrome: A diagnosed neurological condition that encompasses multiple symptoms with a primary focus on extensive levels of fatigue.

Raynaud's Syndrome: A diagnosed syndrome that causes small arteries to narrow leading to poor circulation and temperature regulation, usually peripherally.

Veganism: Not consuming foods and using products that have derived from animals.

*I recognise that a lot of these words and phrases may mean different things to different people depending on your experience, culture, lifestyle, background etc.

However, in this book, I refer to these words/ phrases in the above context

Acknowledgments

Firstly, thank you to my parents: Diane and Sterling, as well as my partner Sam, for always offering continued support throughout my life-long journey. For providing honest, true, and unconditional love, strength, and hope- especially through the tough times. Also, for helping me grow, learn, and find the funny side of life's challenges!

Thank you to my beautiful friends (you know who you are!) that have always offered a listening ear, enjoyed being guinea pigs in my up and coming creations, and stuck by my life decisions throughout this journey.

Thank you to 'Lyndsay' at my local health store, for first introducing me into this world and sharing your incredible journey with me, inspiring me to live my life in such a freeing and beautiful way. It truly opened my eyes.

Thank you to the wider community (too many inspirational people to name!) for offering a plant-based space with accessible resources, food and drink, and increasing communication on the health and ethical benefits of plant-based living.

Thank you to my beautiful baby sprocker spaniel Kenny- for always welcoming me with a smile and a cuddle in times of need, as well as being just as crazy as I am!

And finally- thank you to myself for my dedication, strength, and for never giving up.

Printed in Great Britain
by Amazon

27403772R00057